Sara Swan Miller

Snakes and Lizards

What They Have in Common

Franklin Watts - A Division of Grolier Publishing
New York • London • Hong Kong • Sydney • Danbury, Connecticut

For Mother
You said you like them!

Photographs ©: A. B. Sheldon: 1, 5 bottom right, 7 bottom, 43; NHPA: 30, 31 (Daniel Heuclin); Peter Arnold Inc.: 42 (John Cancalosi), 35 (Doug Cheeseman), 27 (R. Andrew Odum); Photo Researchers: 5 bottom left (John M. Burnley), 19 (Suzanne L. & Joseph T. Collins), 39 (E. R. Degginger), 41 (A. B. Joyce), 29 (Peter B. Kaplan), 25, 33 (Tom McHugh), 17 (Anthony Merceca), 36, 37 (David T. Roberts), 5 top left (Nature's Image Inc./David M. Schleser), 7 top (Dan Suzio); Tony Stone Images: cover, 5 top right (Rod Planck); Visuals Unlimited: 23 (D. Cavagnaro), 6 (Nathan W. Cohen), 13 (Cheryl A. Ertelt), 20, 21 (Joe McDonald), 15 (Rob Simpson).

Illustrations by Jose Gonzales and Steve Savage

The photo on the cover of this book shows a yellow-headed collard lizard.
The photo on the title page shows a timber rattlesnake.

Visit Franklin Watts on the Internet at:
http://publishing.grolier.com

Library of Congress Cataloging-in-Publication Data

Miller, Sara Swan
Snakes and lizards: what they have in common / Sara Swan Miller.
        p. cm. — (Animals in order)
    Includes bibliographical references and index.
    Summary: An introduction to snakes and lizards that includes descriptions of fourteen species and recommendations for finding, identifying, and observing them.
    ISBN 0-531-11594-1 (lib. bdg.)   0-531-16448-9 (pbk.)
    1. Snakes—Juvenile literature. 2. Lizards—Juvenile literature. [1. Snakes 2. Lizards] I. Title. II. Series.
QL666.06M635   2000
597.95—dc21
                                                      99-30417
                                                      CIP
                                                      AC

Contents

Is That a Snake or a Lizard?

At first glance, a snake and a lizard seem quite different. A snake slithers along the ground on its belly. A lizard runs around on four feet. Believe it or not, though, snakes and lizards have a lot in common. That is why scientists have placed them in the same group, or *order*, of animals.

All snakes and lizards have scales covering their bodies. Of course, snakes and lizards are not the only animals with scales. Other *reptiles* have scales too. Snakes and lizards are grouped together because they also have other things in common. Can you guess what some of them are?

Compare the four reptiles shown on the next page. Can you figure out how turtles and alligators are different from snakes and lizards?

Milksnake

Horned lizard

Box turtle

American alligator

Traits of Snakes and Lizards

Of course, it's obvious that snakes and lizards don't have a shell like a turtle. Their jaws are different, too. Turtles have a beak for grabbing food, while snakes and lizards have teeth that grow right out of their jawbones.

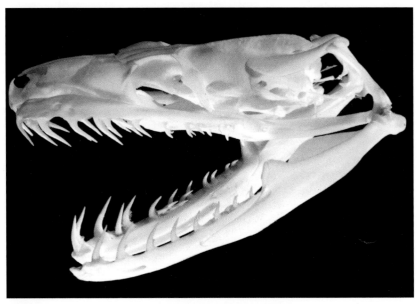

This boa constrictor skull shows the snake's jawbones and teeth.

The teeth and jaws of alligators are different from those of snakes, lizards, and turtles.

Most reptiles lay their eggs on land. The shells of the eggs are tough and leathery, so they won't dry out. The eggs of some snakes and lizards hatch while they're still inside the mother. Some snakes and lizards don't even make eggs. Their young simply grow inside the mother's body.

Like other reptiles, snakes and lizards are *cold-blooded*—their body temperature changes with the temperature of the air around them. When it is cold, they bask in the sun to warm up. When it is hot, they hide in the shade to cool down. You are *warm-blooded*. As long

A female corn snake with her eggs

as you stay healthy, your body temperature will be about 98.6 degrees Fahrenheit (37° Celsius).

Snakes and lizards are always flicking out their tongues. That is how these reptiles smell. When a snake or lizard presses the tip of its tongue to the roof of its mouth, small particles from the air are transferred to a special sense organ in the animal's mouth. Then a message from its brain tells the animal if food—or an enemy—is nearby.

A bull snake uses its tongue to smell.

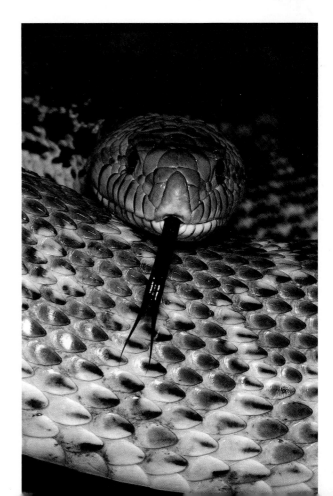

The Order of Living Things

A tiger has more in common with a house cat than with a daisy. A true bug is more like a butterfly than a jellyfish. Scientists arrange living things into groups based on how they look and how they act. A tiger and a house cat belong to the same group, but a daisy belongs to a different group.

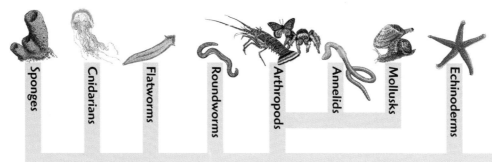

Sponges | Cnidarians | Flatworms | Roundworms | Arthropods | Annelids | Mollusks | Echinoderms

Animals

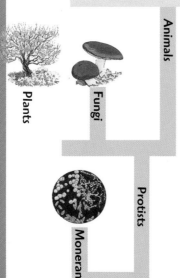

Plants | Fungi

Protists

Monerans

All living things can be placed in one of five groups called *kingdoms*: the plant kingdom, the animal kingdom, the fungus kingdom, the moneran kingdom, or the protist kingdom. You can probably name many of the creatures in the plant and animal kingdoms. The fungus kingdom includes mushrooms, yeasts, and molds. The moneran and protist kingdoms contain thousands of living things that are too small to see without a microscope.

8

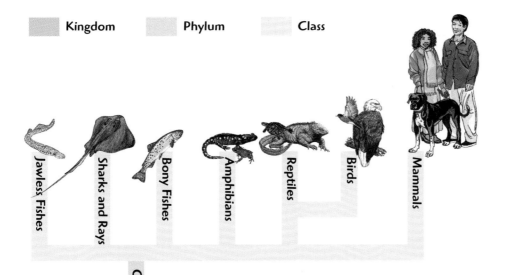

Kingdom　　Phylum　　Class

Jawless Fishes

Sharks and Rays

Bony Fishes

Amphibians

Reptiles

Birds

Mammals

Chordates

Because there are millions and millions of living things on Earth, some of the members of one kingdom may not seem all that similar. The animal kingdom includes creatures as different as tarantulas and trout, jellyfish and jaguars, salamanders and sparrows, elephants and earthworms.

To show that an elephant is more like a jaguar than an earthworm, scientists further separate the creatures in each kingdom into more specific groups. The animal kingdom can be divided into nine *phyla*. Humans belong to the chordate phylum. Almost all chordates have a backbone.

Each phylum can be subdivided into many *classes*. Humans, mice, and elephants all belong to the *mammal* class. Each class can be further divided into orders, orders into *families*, families into *genera*, and genera into *species*. All the members of a species are very similar.

How Snakes and Lizards Fit In

You can probably guess that snakes and lizards belong to the animal kingdom. They have much more in common with tarantulas and turtles than with maple trees and morning glories.

Snakes and lizards belong to the chordate phylum. Almost all chordates have a backbone and a skeleton. Can you think of other chordates? Examples include elephants, mice, alligators, frogs, birds, fish, and whales.

All reptiles belong to the same class. There are three different orders of reptiles. Snakes and lizards make up one of these orders. The scientific name for this order is *squamata*, which comes from a Latin word meaning "scaly."

Snakes and lizards can be divided into a number of different families and genera. These groups can be broken down into thousands of fascinating species.

Snakes and lizards live on every continent except Antarctica so wherever you live, you are sure to come across them. You will learn more about some of the snakes and lizards in this book.

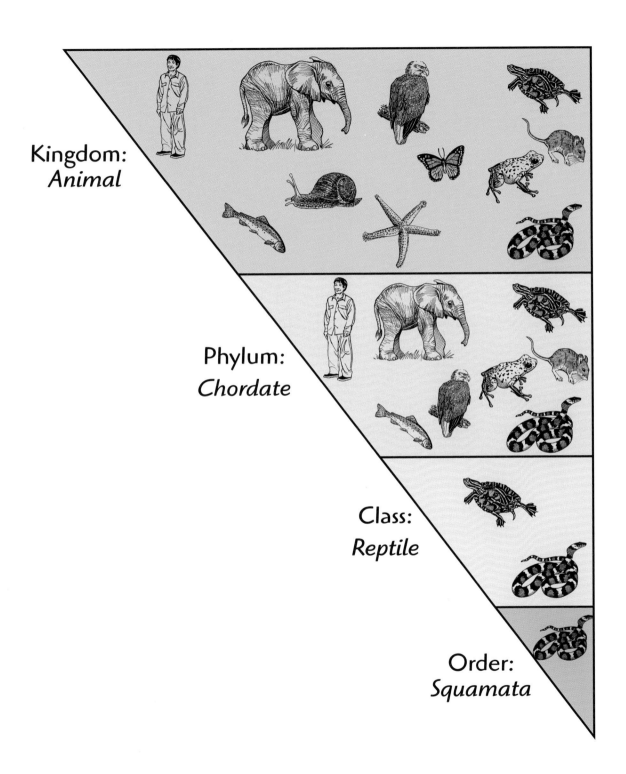

Kingdom:
Animal

Phylum:
Chordate

Class:
Reptile

Order:
Squamata

Rattlesnakes

FAMILY: Viperidae
EXAMPLE: Timber rattlesnake
GENUS AND SPECIES: *Crotalus horridus*
SIZE: 3 to 6 feet (1 to 2 m)

A timber rattlesnake lies coiled up next to a log. It rests its head on the log and waits. Suddenly, it feels the log shake a bit. A small animal is nearby. The snake has small dents on the sides of its head. These pit organs sense the animal's heat. A moment later, the snake sees its *prey*—a mouse. The rattler lunges forward, grabs the mouse with its teeth, and slowly swallows it whole. The snake won't have to eat again for a few days.

In the spring and fall, a timber rattler spends most of its time sunning itself outside its rocky den. If you surprise it, the snake may just slither away into the rocks. But if you're too close, it will rattle its tail loudly. Pay attention! This is a warning to stay away.

When a rattlesnake bites another animal, liquid *venom* flows into the body of its prey. The poison from a rattlesnake bite can kill a person unless he or she is treated right away.

Timber rattlers mate in the late spring. They do not lay eggs. The females give birth to 12-inch (30-cm)-long babies in the late summer or early fall. The young snakes must hurry to find food and a place to spend the winter.

A female rattlesnake does not eat when she's carrying young in her body, so she mates only every other year. She needs the time off to eat, rest, and get her strength back.

Milksnakes

FAMILY: Colubridae
COMMON NAME: Milksnake
GENUS AND SPECIES: *Lampropeltis triangulum*
SIZE: 14 to 78 inches (35 to 198 cm)

Do you know how milksnakes got their name? Farmers who found them in their barns thought the snakes were there to drink milk from the cows. But that's not why milksnakes like barns. They are looking for mice to eat. Mice are often found in barns because they eat the corn and grains that farmers feed cattle.

Milksnakes sleep during the day, and come out at night when the mice are running about. These harmless snakes actually help farmers by eating the mice.

A milksnake's shiny body is covered with a pattern of colored rings or blotches. A milksnake looks a lot like a poisonous copperhead snake. This helps protect the milksnake. Owls and other enemies leave the milksnake alone because they think it is poisonous.

A milksnake has another way to protect itself. When it's scared, it shakes its tail rapidly and makes a rattling sound. Sometimes an enemy thinks it's a rattlesnake and hurries away.

Some scientists think that the rattling noise may sound like a chirping cricket to a hungry mouse. So when the mouse comes looking for dinner, it ends up being the milksnake's main course!

14

Horned Lizards

FAMILY: Iguanidae
COMMON EXAMPLE: Coast horned lizard
GENUS AND SPECIES: *Phrynosoma coronatum*
SIZE: 2 1/2 to 6 3/8 inches (6 to 16 cm)

If an enemy surprises a coast horned lizard, it will surprise the enemy right back! First, it blows itself up with air. It is trying to look big, fierce, and hard to swallow. Then, it opens its mouth and hisses loudly.

If the *predator* hasn't already run away, the lizard squirts two streams of blood from the corners of its eyes. That should startle any enemy! While the enemy is distracted, the lizard can run away and hide.

Finding horned lizards isn't easy. Their squat, tannish-gray bodies blend in with the sandy desert floor. The best place to look for these lizards is near ant mounds. Ants are a horned lizard's favorite food.

In the spring, horned lizards begin their mating game. First, they bob their heads up and down, up and down. Then they do a few push-ups. After they mate, the female wanders off to find a good place to build a nest. She digs a long tunnel and lays up to twenty-one eggs. Then she covers the nest with sand.

When the eggs hatch, the 2-inch (5-cm)-long babies dig their way out. Then they head for the nearest ant mound and look for their first meal.

Glass Lizards

FAMILY: Anguidae
COMMON EXAMPLE: Slender glass lizard
GENUS AND SPECIES: *Ophisaurus attenuatus*
SIZE: 22 to 42 inches (56 to 107 cm)

If you ever see a glass lizard, you will probably think it's a snake. That's because it's a long, skinny creature with no legs! So if it looks like a snake and it slithers like a snake, why do scientists call it a lizard? Like other lizards, it has ear openings on the sides of its head and eyelids that open and close. If you could look at a glass lizard's skeleton, you would see small leg stumps.

Glass lizards are covered with shiny scales. Bony armor inside their scales helps protect them from enemies. This armor makes them very stiff. In fact, it would be hard for them to breathe if they didn't have a line of soft scales running down both sides of their body. The soft scales let them expand their bodies enough to breathe air into their lungs.

Do you know how the glass lizard got its name? If an enemy grabs one by the tail, the tail shatters into pieces—just like glass. Then, while its predator is confused, the lizard quickly crawls away.

The lizard will grow a new tail in just a few weeks. Then it can play the same trick on another hungry predator.

Constrictors

FAMILY: Boidae
COMMON EXAMPLE: Anaconda
GENUS AND SPECIES: *Eunectes murinus*
SIZE: Up to 30 feet (9 m)

In a swamp in South America, a huge anaconda lies just below the water's surface. Only its eyes and nostrils show. When a young tapir comes to take a drink, the anaconda lunges! It grabs the tapir with its teeth and wraps itself around the helpless animal. The anaconda squeezes its prey until the animal stops breathing.

The snake unhinges its jaws and slowly swallows the tapir whole. The tapir makes a huge bulge in the anaconda's belly. After a meal like that, the snake won't need to eat again for months.

Anacondas are among the longest and largest snakes in the world. Their bodies are bigger around than a telephone pole. Many people are afraid of these huge snakes, but they rarely attack humans. Most of the time, they eat birds, fish, and *rodents*. They may also eat deer, wild pigs, and even small crocodiles. An ana-

conda can wrap itself around a crocodile, pin it to a tree, squeeze it to death, and swallow it whole.

Young anacondas hatch inside their mother's body and are born ready to hunt. Each baby is about 3 feet (1 m) long. A mother anaconda often gives birth to many snakes at the same time. Scientists have seen a 19-foot (6-m)-long female give birth to seventy-two babies at once!

Iguanas

FAMILY: Iguanidae

COMMON EXAMPLE: Marine iguana

GENUS AND SPECIES: *Amblyrhynchus cristatus*

SIZE: Up to 4 1/2 feet (1.5 m)

Marine iguanas live along the coastal rocks of the Galapagos Islands off the coast of South America. These large lizards look ferocious, but they won't hurt you. They never attack people. In fact, they don't eat animals. They eat seaweed and *algae*.

Marine iguanas are the only lizards that find their food in the ocean. Marine iguanas are excellent swimmers. They glide through big waves and strong ocean currents. A large male can dive up to 49 feet (15 m) deep. They can stay underwater for 5 to 10 minutes. Some iguanas can stay underwater for as long as an hour.

Ocean water is always colder than the air, so a marine iguana's body temperature can drop 10°F (5°C) when it is underwater. These animals need to take plenty of time to warm up before they dive in. Marine iguanas spend most of the day basking in the sun. They rest on the rocks at the edge of the ocean until they are warmed through. Then they take the plunge into the chilly water.

Egg-eating Snakes

FAMILY: Dasypeltinae

COMMON EXAMPLE: Common egg-eating snake

GENUS AND SPECIES: *Dasypeltis scabra*

SIZE: 30 to 36 inches (76 to 91 cm)

The head of an egg-eating snake is half the size of a chicken egg, but the snake can eat the egg whole. Watching an egg-eating snake devour its meal is an amazing experience.

When an egg-eating snake finds an egg, it flicks its tongue several times. The snake is smelling the egg to make sure it isn't rotten. Then the snake pushes the egg against its body and works its mouth over the egg. It may take 20 minutes for the snake to get the entire egg in its mouth. By that time, the snake's skin is stretched paper-thin.

The egg slowly moves down to the back of the snake's throat. Then the snake arches its neck, so that the pegs at the top of its backbone crack the egg. The snake then sucks down the egg white and yolk, and spits out the shell. Not even an egg-eating snake likes eating eggshells!

Egg-eating snakes spend most of their time in trees, so its easy for them to find birds' eggs. They use their sense of smell to find them.

These snakes are always on the lookout for enemies. Two other snakes—the boomslang and the vine snake—like the taste of egg-

eating snakes. People sometimes kill egg-eaters because they look like a poisonous snake called the night adder. But egg-eating snakes are harmless—unless you're an egg.

Chameleons

FAMILY: Chamaeleonidae
COMMON EXAMPLE: Jackson's chameleon
GENUS AND SPECIES: *Chamaeleo jacksoni*
SIZE: 10 to 13 inches (25 to 33 cm)

A Jackson's chameleon waits in a tree in an African forest. Its toes and tail are wrapped around a branch. Its popping eyes turn separately to search the surroundings. One eye looks forward, while the other looks back.

Suddenly, the chameleon spots a fly. In a flash, it shoots out its long, sticky tongue and grabs the insect! This lizard's tongue is so long that it can catch an insect several inches away. Some chameleons have a tongue as long as their body.

Chameleons can change the color of their skin. People used to think they change color to match their surroundings. Now we know that their color changes when they sense danger or when the temperature or amount of light changes. When a chameleon is partly in the shade and partly in the sunlight, its body is two colors at once— half brown and half green.

A chameleon is a strange-looking animal. Sharp spines run down its back, and its legs are long and thin. Its toes are divided, so its feet look like tiny hands. Other lizards cling to branches with their claws, but a chameleon uses its toes. It can roll its tail up in a curl. You could never mistake a chameleon for anything else!

26

Cobras

FAMILY: Elapidae
COMMON EXAMPLE: King cobra
GENUS AND SPECIES: *Ophiophagus hannali*
SIZE: 12 to 18 feet (4 to 5.5 m)

In a city in India, a snake charmer sits in front of a basket with his legs crossed. He takes off the lid and begins to play his flute. Slowly, a king cobra raises its large, hooded head out of the basket. It stares at the snake charmer and begins swaying back and forth. Is it really dancing to the music?

Actually, a cobra can't even hear music. It comes out because the snake charmer takes off the lid and jiggles the basket. It sways because it's following the snake charmer's swaying body.

The snake charmer must be careful. The king cobra is the largest poisonous snake in the world, and its venom is very powerful. Unlike most snakes, its fangs are always erect and ready to strike. Sometimes it strikes without warning.

A cobra strikes by raising itself up and then falling forward. If it strikes a person, it usually bites below the knee. So you can protect yourself from a cobra by wearing high boots.

King cobras don't like being around people anyway. They live on the plains of India, southeast Asia, and the Philippine Islands. There they hunt for small mammals, birds, and other snakes.

Whipsnakes

FAMILY: Colubridae
COMMON EXAMPLE: Western whipsnake
GENUS AND SPECIES: *Coluber viridiflavus*
SIZE: 3 to 6 1/2 feet (1 to 2 m)

A whipsnake can really whip along! When one of these snakes is in a hurry, it wiggles its body in quick S-shaped loops. The whipsnake is one of the speediest snakes in the world. It can travel up to 4 miles (6.4 km) per hour. This snake's quick turns make it look as though it's going even faster. Predators have a hard time catching a whipsnake.

When it isn't in a hurry, the whipsnake slips along in a straight line like other snakes. It presses its body to the ground, and uses the scales on its belly to help it move along. This snake's scales are sort of like the treads on a tire.

All whipsnakes are very active. They zip along the ground after their prey. They hunt lizards, other snakes, voles, mice, and grasshoppers. They even slither up trees and search for baby birds chirping in their nests.

Like most snakes, whipsnakes lay their eggs in the spring. The females do not stay and protect the eggs. They let the sunshine keep the eggs warm until they hatch.

Whipsnakes are members of the largest family of snakes, the *colubrids*. Three-quarters of the world's snakes are in this family, including the snakes you probably know best—the garter snakes.

Dracos

FAMILY: Agamidae
COMMON EXAMPLE: Flying dragon
GENUS AND SPECIES: *Draco maculatus*
SIZE: 10 to 13 inches (25 to 33 cm)

Who invented hang gliding? It had to be the flying dragon! This small lizard has folds of skin on each side of its skinny body. When it leaps from a branch, the brightly colored folds spread out like wings. Then the flying lizard can glide from tree to tree.

These lizards have another use for their beautiful wings. To attract a female, the males open and close their wings, showing off their brilliant colors. The female chooses one lizard as a mate. She lays her eggs on the ground. When the eggs hatch, the tiny babies scramble up the nearest tree as fast as they can.

This lizard is very good at hiding from enemies. When it races along the ground or climbs a tree, its folds of skin lie flat. This helps the lizard blend in with its surroundings. When it stretches out its head, legs, and long tail, a flying lizard looks just like the twig it is lying on.

Flying lizards seem to like each other's company. They often travel in small groups. They climb up tree trunks and search for ants to eat. When they get to the top, they leap off together and glide down to the base of another tree. Watch out, ants!

Monitors

FAMILY: Varanidae
COMMON EXAMPLE: Komodo dragon
GENUS AND SPECIES: *Varanus komodoensis*
SIZE: Up to 10 feet (3 m)

The Komodo dragon is enormous! It can grow 10 feet (3 m) long and weigh as much as 300 pounds (136 kg). It's amazing that no one discovered this huge lizard until about 100 years ago.

Many people tell stories about how ferocious Komodo dragons are, but they're not really that fierce. They would rather scare an enemy than fight. If a Komodo dragon is cornered, it puffs up its body, hisses loudly, and swings its long tail back and forth.

If it hits an enemy with its powerful tail, it could hurt. When a Komodo dragon is really scared, it will bite an attacker. These lizards have very strong jaws.

Komodo dragons like to feed on dead animals. If they can't find any dead creatures, they hunt for live prey. Even a deer or a wild hog is not too big for a Komodo dragon to attack. When the animal is dead, the lizard tears off big chunks of meat and swallows them whole.

Komodo dragons can run quickly and swim well. They often climb trees, too. When they want to rest, they dig a burrow and hide inside.

Seasnakes

FAMILY: Hydrophidae
COMMON EXAMPLE: Yellow-bellied seasnake
GENUS AND SPECIES: *Pelamis platurus*
SIZE: Up to 3 1/4 feet (1 m)

The yellow-bellied seasnake spends its whole life in the ocean. The sides of its body are flat, so it can swim fast. Its nostrils are on the top of its head, and it can close them off when it is underwater.

This seasnake can stay underwater for a long time because it has one, very large *lung* that is almost as long as its body. When it does come up for air, the yellow-bellied seasnake can breathe in air without lifting its head all the way out of the water.

Some seasnakes come up onto land to lay eggs, but yellow-bellied babies grow inside their mother's body. She gives birth to her young right in the water. That's because this seasnake can't stay on land long. It has no scales on its belly to help it slither along the ground.

Yellow-bellied seasnakes are poisonous. They hunt fish and eels. Their venom is so poisonous that eels die just a few seconds after they are bitten. Yellow-bellied seasnakes don't usually bite swimmers, but if you ever find one washed up on shore, stay away!

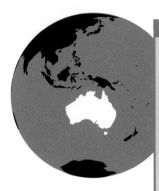

Elapids

FAMILY: Elapidae
COMMON EXAMPLE: Tiger snake
GENUS AND SPECIES: *Notechis scutatus*
SIZE: Up to 8 feet (2.5 m)

Can you guess how tiger snakes got their name? Most of them are brown with yellow stripes, like a tiger. Some tiger snakes have very few stripes, and come in other colors—yellow, orange, olive, brown, or black.

The tiger snake is very common in Australia. It has the most powerful venom of any land snake. If a tiger snake's venom *glands* were as big as a rattlesnake's, they would carry enough poison to kill 400 people!

Tiger snakes are easily annoyed, so sometimes they bite people. Before a tiger snake strikes, it flattens its head and neck, raises the front of its body, and sways back and forth. This is one snake you want to stay away from!

Most tiger snakes live in swamps. They hunt for prey along the ground or in the bushes. The prey usually dies just a few seconds after the snake bites it.

A female tiger snake carries her eggs inside her body until they hatch. She may give birth to as many as seventy-two young at a time!

Dragon Lizards

FAMILY: Agamidae
COMMON EXAMPLE: Frilled lizard
GENUS AND SPECIES: *Chlamydosaurus kingii*
SIZE: 3 1/4 feet (1 m)

The frilled lizard may be small, but it can give you quite a scare. If you startle one, it will rear up on its back legs. Then it will unfold a huge frill that encircles its head like a brightly colored umbrella. Finally, the lizard opens its mouth wide to show the bright-colored lining. If that doesn't scare you away, it may start hissing and lunge toward you. After that, the lizard will probably turn around and run away.

The frilled lizard isn't as fierce as it seems. When it throws up its frilly collar, it looks twice as big as it really is. The lizard is trying to scare away predators. Suddenly flashing the bright colors of its mouth also startles its enemies.

A frilled lizard usually keeps its collar folded up along its neck. Its brown body blends in with the branch it's sitting on. The lizard waits patiently for a spider or insect to pass by. When it spots prey, the lizard catches it and quickly gobbles it down.

Females lay their eggs in the spring, but they don't stay around to protect them. When the young lizards hatch, they are very small, but they have the same big, gaudy frills to scare off their enemies.

Saving Snakes and Lizards

Some people are fascinated by snakes and lizards. They keep boas, garter snakes, chameleons, and iguanas as pets. Other people think snakes and lizards are slimy and dirty, but they are actually clean animals with dry, scaly skin.

Many people fear snakes and lizards. You might be surprised to learn that less than one-quarter of snakes and only one species of lizard are poisonous. Very few people are bitten by poisonous snakes.

When a snake bite is treated quickly, the victim will probably survive. It isn't easy to tell whether a snake is poisonous, so it is best to leave all snakes alone.

Because people are afraid of snakes, they sometimes kill them without even stopping to think. They don't realize how important these animals are. Snakes and lizards eat rodents that invade our homes and insects that destroy plants.

These girls aren't scared of snakes.

They are also a source of food for many different kinds of birds and mammals. Like all animals, snakes and lizards have a place in the balance of nature.

Many species of snakes and lizards are threatened or endangered today. People have killed them out of fear or to make their skins into shoes, handbags, and clothing. In some parts of the world, people kill these animals for food. Many snakes and lizards have died because their *habitats* were destroyed.

As we learn more about snakes and lizards, we realize how important they are. In recent years, laws have been passed to protect these animals and their environments. Today, many people are working hard to save snakes and lizards. Let's hope these fascinating reptiles can survive!

This purse was made from the skin of an anaconda.

Words to Know

algae—tiny green creatures that grow in water or damp places

class—a group of creatures within a phylum that share certain characteristics

colubrids—the largest family of snakes

cold-blooded—having a body temperature that changes along with the temperature of the animal's surroundings

family—a group of creatures within an order that share certain characteristics

genus (plural **genera**)—a group of creatures within a family that share certain characteristics

gland—an organ in the body that produces and gives off a liquid

habitat—the natural environment of an animal

kingdom—one of the five divisions into which all living things are placed: the animal kingdom, the plant kingdom, the fungus kingdom, the moneran kingdom, and the protist kingdom

lung—an organ that moves air that is breathed in to an animal's blood

mammal—a warm-blood animal that feeds its young with mother's milk and usually has some hair covering its skin

order—a group of creatures within a class that share certain characteristics

phylum (plural **phyla**)—a group of creatures within a kingdom that share certain characteristics

predator—an animal that hunts other animals for food

prey—an animal hunted for food by another animal (a predator)

reptile—a group of animals that are covered with scales and lay eggs on land. Examples include snakes, turtles, crocodiles, and lizards.

rodent—the order of mammals that includes mice, rats, squirrels, voles, shrews, and chipmunks

species—a group of creatures within a genus that share certain characteristics. Members of a species can mate and produce young.

squamata—the order of animals that includes snakes and lizards

venom—a poison that animals use to catch prey or fight enemies

warm-blooded—having a body temperature that is internally regulated. Humans are warm-blooded and maintain a body temperature close to 98.6°F (37°C).

Learning More

Books

Burns, Diane. *Take-Along Guide to Snakes, Salamanders, and Lizards.* Minocqua, WI: Northwood Press, 1995.

Conant, Roger. *Peterson's First Guide to Reptiles and Amphibians.* Boston: Houghton Mifflin, 1992.

Lovett, Sarah. *Extremely Weird Reptiles.* Santa Fe: John Muir Publications, 1996.

Smith, Hobart and Howard S. Zimm. *Golden Guide to Reptiles and Amphibians.* New York: Golden Press, 1987.

Snedden, Robert. *What Is a Reptile?* San Fransisco: Sierra Club Books, 1995.

Web Sites

Anatomy of a Snake
http://herpetology.com/anatomy.html
This site features a labeled diagram of a snake's body parts.

Geckoland
http://members.xoom.com/geckoland/
This site answers all your questions about geckos and how to care for them.

Kingsnake & Milksnake Page
http://www.kingsnake.com/king/
Learn all about these snakes, and see photographs of them. This site includes instructions for caring for snakes of the genus *Lampropeltis*.

Index

About the Author

Sara Swan Miller has enjoyed working with children all her life, first as a nursery-school teacher, and later as an outdoor environmental educator at the Mohonk Preserve in New Paltz, New York. As the director of the Preserve school program, she has led hundreds of children on field trips and taught them the importance of appreciating and respecting the natural world.

She has written a number of children's books, including *Three Stories You Can Read to Your Dog*; *Three Stories You Can Read to Your Cat*; *What's in the Woods? An Outdoor Activity Book*; *Oh, Cats of Camp Rabbitbone!*; *Piggy in the Parlor and Other Tales*; *Better Than TV*; and *Will You Sting Me? Will You Bite? The Truth About Some Scary-Looking Insects*. She has also written many other books for the Animals in Order series.